the Weekend Crafter®

Soapmaking

the Weekend Crafter®

Soapmaking

20 Terrific
Melt & Pour Projects

JOANNE O'SULLIVAN

LARK BOOKS

A Division of Sterling Publishing Co., Inc.
New York

PROJECT DESIGNERS:
ALLISON SMITH
TERRY TAYLOR

ART DIRECTOR & PRODUCTION:
MEGAN KIRBY
KATHLEEN HOLMES

PHOTOGRAPHER:
EVAN BRACKEN

COVER DESIGNER:
BARBARA ZARETSKY

PRODUCTION ASSISTANCE:
LORELEI BUCKLEY

EDITORIAL ASSISTANCE:
DELORES GOSNELL

Library of Congress Cataloging-in-Publication Data

O'Sullivan, Joanne.
　　Soapmaking : 20 terrific melt & pour projects / by Joanne O'Sullivan.—1st ed.
　　　　p.　cm. — (The weekend crafter)
　　Includes index.
　　ISBN 1-57990-372-X (paper)
　　1. Soap.　I. Title.　　II. Series.

　TP991 .078 2003
　668'.12—dc21

　　　　　　　　　　　　　　　2002034354

10 9 8 7 6 5 4 3 2 1

First Edition

Published by Lark Books, a division of
Sterling Publishing Co., Inc.
387 Park Avenue South, New York, N.Y. 10016

© 2003, Lark Books

Distributed in Canada by Sterling Publishing,
c/o Canadian Manda Group, One Atlantic Ave., Suite 105
Toronto, Ontario, Canada M6K 3E7

Distributed in the U.K. by Guild of Master Craftsman Publications Ltd., Castle
Place, 166 High Street, Lewes, East Sussex, England BN7 1XU
Tel: (+ 44) 1273 477374, Fax: (+ 44) 1273 478606, Email: pubs@thegmcgroup.com,
Web: www.gmcpublications.com

Distributed in Australia by Capricorn Link (Australia) Pty Ltd.,
P.O. Box 704, Windsor, NSW 2756 Australia

If you have questions or comments about this book, please contact:
Lark Books
67 Broadway
Asheville, NC 28801
(828) 253-0467
Printed in China

ISBN 1-57990-372-x

CONTENTS

INTRODUCTION

AT THE END OF a stressful day, a warm bath with an appealing bar of handmade soap is one of the most relaxing rituals imaginable. Soap is a necessity, but a special handcrafted soap is one of life's little luxuries. Beyond leaving you squeaky clean and refreshed, it can clear your head, soothe your skin, and lift your spirits. A handmade soap is a wonderful gift, but you don't have to wait until you receive one to start enjoying this simple bath time indulgence. You can easily make your own with just a few materials, a little time, and the know-how this book provides.

In the past, soapmaking was time-consuming and messy—a complicated process better left to those with experience. With new materials available, such as glycerin melt-and-pour soap base, anyone can make soap in less than an hour, no experience necessary. Making melt and pour soap is like simple cooking. You use a microwave oven (or double boiler and stovetop if you don't have one) and ordinary kitchen supplies, such as a knife, cutting board, and microwave-safe container. You may not need to purchase anything except glycerin soap base, which you can find on-line or at craft stores. You don't need special skills to get started—just your own imagination and the guidelines we provide. Following six basic steps, you can create a soap that's ready to use within an hour. If you make mistakes while you're learning, you can just melt down your soap and start all over again.

Melt and pour soapmaking is an art and a craft—a great opportunity for creativity. Handmade soaps artfully blend shape, color, fragrance, and texture. There are countless ways to express a mood or evoke a sensation by combining these different elements in a soap. Create a colorful bar that's perfect as a morning pick-me-up or make a soothing soap that restores moisture after a day in the sun. Experienced crafters and beginners alike will find melt and pour soapmaking an easy, satisfying way to create something that's both beautiful and functional.

In the Getting Started section of the book, we'll introduce you to the basic supplies you need for melt and pour soapmaking, and walk you through the process step-by-step. We even include ideas on how to wrap your finished soap. You'll find advice on choosing colors and scents for you soaps, as well as a troubleshooting guide to help you identify common flaws that may appear in finished soap projects.

The Projects section of the book features a range of projects to suit your style and skill level. From simple soaps in novelty molds to layered soaps with botanical additives, you'll find a variety of inspirational ideas. We've included soaps with elements that exfoliate or add moisture, as well as those that are purely decorative. Follow our instructions or adapt the recipes to create soaps with your own choice of colors, scents, and shapes. Since no two molds are alike, our instructions leave the measurements up to you. Experiment with your materials and molds to find out what works for you.

Pamper yourself and your friends with melt and pour soaps that make bathing a pleasure. You'll be surprised how quickly you'll become an expert and produce professional looking results.

GETTING STARTED

Basic Supplies

Melt and pour soapmaking is a low-investment, low-risk craft. You may be able to get started without buying a single piece of equipment. Basic kitchen tools and utensils are all you need for the simple mixing and melting you'll do. When you're ready to pour the soap, you'll need a mold, but you might be able to use what's in your kitchen for that, too. The following list outlines the tools and supplies you should have on hand before you start a project.

MICROWAVE OVEN

For all the projects in this book, a microwave oven is used to melt the soap base, the primary material of melt and pour soap. Every make and model of microwave is different, so you'll need to experiment with yours to find out how your soap base reacts to its settings—some will melt more quickly than others. If you don't have a microwave, you can use cooking pots arranged for the double-boiler method of melting (see page 13).

KITCHENWARE AND UTENSILS

For many simple projects, you won't need everything on the following list: only a microwave-safe container and a stirring implement. For more specialized projects, you may need to add a few items, but they're generally things you can find in your kitchen. You may want to keep your soapmaking supplies separate from the utensils you use for cooking. Although soap washes off easily, it's better to be on the safe side in case any residue remains after you've cleaned the supplies.

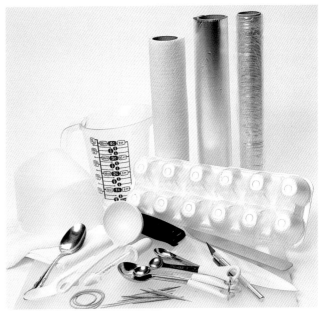

Basic melt-and-pour soapmaking supplies

Basic List

❏ Sharp knife
❏ Butter knife or table knife
❏ Washable cutting board
❏ Measuring cups and spoons
❏ Microwave-safe bowls
❏ Glass mixing bowls
❏ Spoon or other stirring implement
❏ Eyedroppers for adding color (optional)
❏ Grater or grinder (optional)
❏ Cosmetic-grade sprayer*
❏ Dishtowels, rags, or egg carton for stabilizing molds

*You can use a plant sprayer, but you'll have better luck with a cosmetic-grade sprayer, which can be found in the cosmetics section of drugstores.

Extras for Specialized Projects

❏ Ladle
❏ Small funnel
❏ Aluminum foil
❏ Rubber bands

MOLDS

Choosing your mold is the first step in your soap design process. Do you want to make a single soap or create a whole loaf that you can slice into multiple bars? Do you want a simple or a distinctive shape? A three-dimensional or a flat soap?

You can purchase molds made especially for soapmaking, or borrow from molds made for other crafts, such as candle and candy-making. Metal baking tins and molds, cookie cutters, ice cube trays, frozen dessert molds, and microwave-safe plastic containers make good soap molds and you can probably find them right there in your kitchen cabinets. You can even create makeshift molds from aluminum foil. Don't forget to look in your garage or basement too. PVC pipes are perfect tube

A variety of molds

molds because they're inexpensive and withstand high temperatures. You'll just need to cover one end with aluminum foil and rubber bands to keep the melted soap base from leaking out.

There are several criteria to consider when choosing a mold. First, is the mold safe for use with high temperatures? It will need to withstand the heat of the melted soap base and the dishwasher without melting or buckling. Next, is the mold flexible? There's a fine line between flexible and flimsy. You'll need a mold that holds liquid without spilling, yet is not so rigid that you need to bang it to get the soap out. After all, the soap won't do you much good if you can't get it out of the mold.

The material a mold is made from determines how easy it is to use. Plastic or resin are ideal materials for soap molds. Rubber or liquid latex are also effective. You may long to use a particular traditional wooden cookie mold, but its lack of flexibility may cause problems when it's time to get the soap out. Glass and ceramic items don't make good molds either. You can try metal molds, but look for those that are somewhat flexible.

Once you've determined the material you'll use, consider the shape. Many beginner soapcrafters start out with a loaf mold to create one big soap block that can be cut into slices. If you want to make a soap with different layers in one bar or loaf, use a clear mold so you can see how each layer interacts with the other and observe any additives you put in to ensure they end up where you want them. Try to avoid a mold that already has a texture—even a subtle one will show up on the surface of your soap.

Mold Release

With most molds (especially those made specifically for soapmaking), you'll simply need to press on the sides of the mold and the soap will pop right out. If you do have trouble removing your soap from a mold, you may want to try a mold release, a substance that serves to lubricate the mold. A vegetable oil spray (used for cooking) is one option that works well—spray the mold before pouring in your soap. Some soapcrafters prefer using petroleum jelly. Try both and see what works for you.

Spraying your mold with a vegetable oil mold release helps make unmolding easier.

Materials

SOAP BASE

For centuries, soap has been made with lard (an animal fat), tallow (a different kind of animal fat), lye (a by-product of burnt wood ashes), caustic soda (a seaweed by-product), and vegetable or nut oils, such as olive oil, palm oil, or coconut

Clear, white opaque, and olive oil glycerin soap base

oil. The trick to transforming these substances into soap is to combine them in the correct measure, as no single ingredient makes soap on its own. Once mixed with water, heated, and cooled, *saponification* or soap creation takes place. The soap takes time to cure, or settle. This whole process can be quite lengthy and complicated, so until recently soapmaking was a craft undertaken only by the truly dedicated.

Melt and pour soapmaking is a relatively new way of making soap. Unlike traditional lye or fat-based soaps (called cold-process soaps), all melt and pour soaps start out with a *glycerin* base. Glycerin, an alcohol substance that's a by-product of the soapmaking process, can be vegetable-oil based or created synthetically from a petroleum by-product, making it less expensive to produce. It's easy to cut and it melts smoothly and quickly into a (usually) clear, sticky liquid. To this you can add fragrance, color, or other additives. Let the ingredients set for about 30 minutes, and you've got soap. Making soap from melted glycerin takes water out of the soapmaking process. Glycerin makes soapmaking quicker and easier: less mixing and curing time are involved.

Glycerin is usually sold by the pound (454 g) in blocks or bricks, but it's also available in curls or shavings. Whatever the shape, the glycerin is cut up into pieces, melted down, poured into molds, and cooled to create a bar of soap. Because all molds are different, it's difficult to say how many bars of soap you could make with a specific measurement, such as a five-pound (2.2 k) block. On average, you should be able to make about five soaps per pound (454 g) of soap base.

You may be familiar with clear glycerin base, but you're not limited to making clear soap. You can also buy white opaque base (same as clear but with added titanium dioxide, a whitening agent), natural oil base (white coconut or olive oil), or a precolored base, which makes adding colorants unnecessary. You can also find soap base that contains goat's milk, avocado, or cucumber for moisture. By using a white or colored soap base, you can create a soap that looks like a traditional cold-process soap but takes a fraction of the time to make.

You should be able to easily find melt-and-pour glycerin soap base at craft stores or through on-line suppliers. With an overwhelming variety of products to choose from, you may be unsure of what distinguishes each brand of soap base. Even though two products may be sold under the same name, they may vary greatly in composition, so you'll need to do a little research. In soapmaking, it's often true that you get what you pay for. If a manufacturer's soap base costs significantly less than others on the market, it may be because the quality is markedly lower. A poor-quality base will determine the outcome of your final product and you probably won't be satisfied with the results. If you can, buy a small amount of soap base and test it out.

Here are some tips for evaluating the quality of a soap base:

What is it made from? Glycerin that's made from pure vegetable and nut oils is best. With a pure, natural base, your soap is likely to be safe and appropriate for all skin types. Try to avoid using a base that has a lot of additives, such as wax filler and alcohol. Wax filler doesn't have cleansing ability, so it makes your soap less effective and leaves a residue. Alcohol is another additive that makes soap smell better, but it can dry out the skin. How can you tell if your base has a lot of additives? Additives change the color of the base. Look for base that's clear, not cloudy or yellowish.

How does it melt? You're looking for a soap that melts easily, pours smoothly, and doesn't create a lot of bubbles (you'll also get bubbles from overheating your soap).

How does it lather? If you can't work up a good lather with your soap base, it's not going to clean well, which is after all, its purpose.

Does it leave a residue on your skin? You can make the prettiest soap in the world, but if it leaves residue, no one is going to want to use it. Before moving on to aesthetic considerations, make sure the soap does its job.

How does it smell? Your glycerin base should have almost no smell. A base with a strong odor detracts from the fragrance that you want to add. You also want to know how a base "takes" scent. Do a test by adding the same amount of the same fragrance to different types of soap base, then see if the scent is stronger and more sustained in one than in another. Check back after an hour or so after the soap has cooled and set to see if there is any change in the results.

RUBBING ALCOHOL AND SPRAYER

To keep bubbles from forming on the surface of your soap, spray rubbing alcohol on the surface with an oil mister or cosmetic-grade sprayer. Alcohol also helps different layers of soap stick together and may prevent cracks from forming around the embeds (see page 13) in your soap. Just be careful when using alcohol around heat and make sure it doesn't come onto contact with any open flames.

Cosmetic-grade sprayers for rubbing alcohol

FRAGRANCE ADDITIVES

When someone picks up an alluring bar of soap, the first thing they do is smell it. Fragrance can make the difference between an ordinary soap and one that's a delight to use. For a true scented-soap lover, a soap's first duty is to smell good, and there's nothing more disappointing than a bar of soap that's lost its scent. On

Lavendar is a popular fragrance additive.

the other hand, many people, especially those with sensitive skin, may develop skin irritation or allergic reactions when exposed to certain fragrances. If you're creating soap strictly for yourself, you can experiment to your heart's content. If you plan to sell your soap or give it as a gift, keep the recipient in mind. Try creating a range of options—some soaps with fragrance and some without.

One way to add fragrance to a soap is by using herbs (see page 11). Perhaps a more versatile way is to use oils. Two main types of oils are used for adding scent to soap.

Essential oils are pure oils made from plant extracts and can be found at most natural food stores or ordered online. An essential oil provides a very powerful, concentrated scent but may leave a substantial dent in your pocketbook. Since these oils are extracted from flowers and herbs through a very time-consuming process, they're costly to produce, and consequently, costly for the consumer.

A more economical alternative is the *fragrance oil*, a synthetically created oil that uses essential oils as a base, but alters and adds to them. Since fragrance oils are chemically produced, they can blend scents together to make an entirely new aroma. Rather than just a rose scent that would be available in an essential oil, you can purchase a rose-jasmine or rose-gardenia scent. There are hundreds of fragrance oils available, and they're priced much lower than essential oils. The drawback to this kind of oil is that some lower-priced and lower-quality fragrance oils dissipate quickly, leaving only a faint trace of the original scent. If you do use fragrance oils, try to go for higher quality and slightly more expensive products. You'll use less of the oil, and in the long run, your fragrance will last longer.

In addition to essential and fragrance oils, you can use commercial perfumes to scent your soap. For convenience, you may be tempted to use food extracts such as vanilla or almond in your soap. However, these products don't provide much scent and tend to dry out the skin. Candle and potpourri oils may also strike you as a low-cost solution to adding fragrance, but don't try them. They're not designed for the soapmaking process, so they're ineffective, irritating to the skin, and possibly dangerous (because of the high temperatures involved in soapcrafting). Before investing in an unfamiliar fragrance additive, find out if it's considered "cosmetic grade," which means it's safe to use for homemade cosmetics and bath products.

COLOR ADDITIVES

A perfectly clear glycerin soap looks beautiful just as it is, so you may decide that you don't need to add color. If you do decide to add color, you have a range of options. Once again herbs (and spices) are a natural choice (see the following section for more information). But using only herbs limits your color range. You'll find colorants made specifically for soaps on-line and at craft stores. Soap colorants can be found in chips, blocks, liquid, powder, and grated forms. Liquid is the easiest form to use because it dissolves naturally without leaving clumps (the colored soaps in this book were made using either liquid colorant or herbs). As with fragrance, you'll want to use a colorant that's considered cosmetic grade to avoid skin irritation or allergies.

Liquid color additives

While food coloring may seem like a convenient choice because of its wide availability, it's not designed for soap and its drawbacks outweigh its advantages. First, food colors fade quickly. Your soap may start out with a dramatic jewel-tone hue only to fade in a matter of hours. Unless you're looking for just a light hint of color, you probably won't be satisfied with the results. Second, food colors bleed, meaning the color seeps from one part of the soap to another. Finally, food colors may stain washcloths, soap dishes, and vanities. You'll find that using natural or cosmetic-grade colorant helps you to avoid these problems and provides you with consistent, long-lasting color that's safe on the skin.

HERBS, SPICES, AND BOTANICALS

Herbs and botanicals such as flower petals and buds do double duty in a soap: they add both color and fragrance (not to mention texture). You should be able to find a variety of herbs and botanicals at your local natural food store. If you're unsure about the properties of a certain additive, there is usually an expert on hand to answer questions. As with any additive, use caution. Some herbs can be irritating to the skin.

To add scent, choose herbs or botanicals known for their strong fragrance, such as lavender, rosemary, mint, rose petals and hips, chamomile, and calendula flower. You may even want to try something more exotic like lemongrass or nettle. Although herbs can be unpredictable, they usually hold scent well. Most soapcrafters use herbs that are already ground into a powdery form. If you can't find herbs or flowers ground to your liking, you can grind them yourself with a coffee or food grinder. Using sprigs or stems creates a dramatic look. Adding whole buds, however, usually creates a muddy brown look.

To add color using herbs, experiment first. Sometimes it takes a while for the color change to appear in the soap base, and sometimes the color will grow darker or fade as time goes on. One way to test the color change is to make several soaps using the same base and different herbal additives. That way you can see how the additive affects the outcome of the soap. For example, vanilla may color a soap deep taupe, while another botanical may turn it slightly yellow.

In addition to herbs, consider adding spices to your soap. Paprika is often used for its strong red color, which when added to soap creates a deep pinkish color. Turmeric creates a soft yellow, and cocoa powder infuses soap with a warm brown.

Ground herbs add color and fragrance to soap.

OTHER NATURAL ADDITIVES

Beyond looking great, smelling great, and cleansing well, you may want your soap to perform on a higher level. If so, you can add elements that provide moisturizing, astringent, exfoliating, or decorative qualities.

Moisturizing Elements

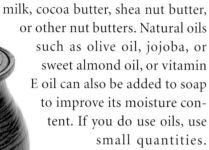

To turn your soap into a moisture bar, add honey, goat's milk, cocoa butter, shea nut butter, or other nut butters. Natural oils such as olive oil, jojoba, or sweet almond oil, or vitamin E oil can also be added to soap to improve its moisture content. If you do use oils, use small quantities. Some will spoil over time unless treated with a preservative. Herbs like calendua flower and chamomile are known as softeners, as are rose petals. Aloe vera gel provides a soap with both moisturizing and healing properties. Some soapcrafters add beeswax to help thicken the soap and support the properties of the additives.

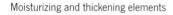
Moisturizing and thickening elements

Exfoliating Elements

Natural additives such as oatmeal, almonds (or almond meal), cornmeal, and ground coffee not only give your soap a nice texture, they gently scrub, slough, and exfoliate the skin. A natural loofah sponge makes a great soap mold and is a great natural exfoliate. Raspberry, strawberry, grape, poppy, or cranberry seeds are other options to try. Pumice has strong exfoliating power but should be used sparingly, as it can be harsh. A better alternative might be sea salt, which gives the skin a good scrub and leaves it glowing. Avoid using harsh exfoliating soaps on the face. They're best used for rough spots like elbows and feet.

Oatmeal, coffee, and tea add astringent qualities to soap.

Astringent Elements

Earth clays draw dirt and oil from the skin.

Astringents remove oil and dirt from your skin, toning and revitalizing the complexion. Earth clays are easy to add to your soap and provide an astringent quality. Some examples of earth clays are green clay (also called French green clay), a detoxifying powder often used in masks; bentonite clay, a by-product of volcanic ash processed to draw oils from the skin; white clay, often used in deodorants and powders to absorb dirt; and red clay, another astringent that revives the skin. Herbal teas and green tea have mild astringent properties, as do seaweed, kelp, tea tree oil, and eucalyptus.

SYNTHETIC AND OTHER ADDITIVES

Beyond the natural additives, there are many artificial additives that give your soap extra sparkle, shine, and dimension.

Pearlescent Powders

Pearlescent powders made especially for use in soap and other cosmetics can be purchased through on-line suppliers and sometimes at beauty supply stores. Gold, white, silver, and copper powders are some examples. You can also find pearlescent pigments that have been added to clear or colored liquids. Cosmetic-grade glitter, which comes in bigger chunks and makes a bigger impact, is another option. Add

Pearlescent powders, glitters, and sequins can be suspended or embedded in soap.

gold or copper leaf to the outside of a soap for a luxurious look. Sparkly sequins add a purely decorative effect.

Embeds

A soap with an embed is like a present within a present. Everyone loves that feeling of having something to keep and enjoy after the soap is gone. Bath toys or charms are popular and useful embeds, but you can also choose an embed to echo the theme of your soap. For example, a soap with orange color and fragrance may have an embedded slice of dried orange, while a flower-shape soap may contain dried or silk flower petals. You may also choose to embed an opaque soap shape inside a clear bar or vice versa.

Melt and Pour Soapmaking: The Basic Technique

Basic melt and pour soapmaking can be explained in six steps. It's an easy process, but that doesn't mean it's without challenges. It takes time, patience, and experience to get comfortable with the process, to learn from your mistakes, and to develop a soapcrafter's intuition. Don't rush through the steps. Build in time for careful mixing of colors and fragrances, adding elements, and letting the soap cool and set. Take it easy, experiment, and get to know your materials.

For the projects in this book, we avoided giving exact measurements. Each mold is different, and soap bases are different too. When you begin to make soap, experiment with measures, always starting out with a relatively small amount of color, fragrance, or other elements, and adding more if needed. If you are planning to one day reproduce your soap, you may want to use specific measurements so you can repeat your creation.

Step 1: Cut Your Soap Base

Cut up your soap base (some brands of soap base come in prescored blocks to make cutting easier). You can cut it into slices or cubes. The smaller your pieces, the more quickly they will melt, so keep them small.

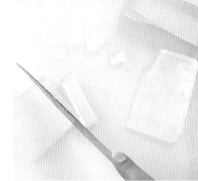

MELTING SOAP IN A DOUBLE BOILER

If you don't have a microwave, or, prefer a stovetop method, use a "double boiler." A double boiler is great for melt and pour soapmaking because it prevents the soap base from getting too hot. Heat the water in the larger pot or pan, then when it's boiling, set your smaller pot of soap base on top of the boiling water.

When melting soap in a double boiler, keep a lid on the pot that contains the base to hold in the moisture and prevent a film from quickly developing on the top of the soap.

Let your soap base start to melt. You can turn down the heat a little to be on the safe side. Once the base is completely melted and simmering, remove it, but keep the lid on the pot until you pour it into the mold.

Determine how much melted soap base you'll need for your particular mold. To do this, use a measuring cup to pour water into your mold. If your mold holds 2 ounces (59.1 ml) of water, it will hold the same amount of melted soap. Cut small pieces of soap base and melt them to determine how many chunks of base you'll need to cut to get that much melted soap. Since you can always melt more base, start out small. Even if you overdo it, you can always remelt the soap and use it again for another project. As you become more experienced you'll get better at estimating how much soap to cut.

Step 2: Melt Your Soap Base

For all the projects in this book, we used a microwave oven to melt the soap base. You can also use a double boiler (see box on page 13 for instructions).

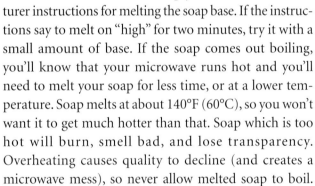

Place your cut base pieces in a microwave-safe container.

The temperature settings on different microwave models vary, so before you begin soapmaking, you'll need to test yours to find out if it runs cool or hot. To do so, simply follow the manufacturer instructions for melting the soap base. If the instructions say to melt on "high" for two minutes, try it with a small amount of base. If the soap comes out boiling, you'll know that your microwave runs hot and you'll need to melt your soap for less time, or at a lower temperature. Soap melts at about 140°F (60°C), so you won't want it to get much hotter than that. Soap which is too hot will burn, smell bad, and lose transparency. Overheating causes quality to decline (and creates a microwave mess), so never allow melted soap to boil.

Experiment with melting your soap base until you figure out the ideal time and temperature. You'd much rather have to put the base back in the microwave for a few minutes than to overheat it. You can start melting and checking in two-minute intervals, then build up to five- or 10-minute intervals. Each time you check, look to see if some pieces remain unmelted. If there are some unmelted clumps, stir very gently or simply "nudge" them with a spoon or stirring implement.

When you remove the melted soap from the microwave, stir it very lightly to make sure it melted evenly and that there are no clumps. If you stir too much, you'll end up with bubbles in your soap that may be difficult to get out and may affect the soap's clarity.

Allow your soap to cool slightly (but not so long that a skin appears on the surface) before pouring to prevent melting or warping your mold.

Step 3: Add Fragrance

Let your melted soap cool momentarily. If you add fragrance to a soap that's too hot, the fragrance will quickly "burn off." Don't wait too long to add it though, as your soap will start to harden.

Start by adding a little scent at a time to test the interaction of your base with the fragrance. A good rule of thumb is to start with ½ to 1 teaspoon (2.5 to 5 ml) of scent per 1 pound (454 g) of soap base. Since you'll use far less than 1 pound (454 g), just add the fragrance drop by drop (another rule of thumb is use one to four drops of scent per ounce [29.5 ml] of soap). If you add fragrance carefully and gradually, you should avoid overscenting it. Wait a moment to let the power of the fragrance hit you before adding more.

Step 4: Add Color

As with fragrance, you'll want to add color gradually, observing how it reacts to the base before proceeding. Eyedroppers are an ideal tool for adding color to your soaps, since they let you release color one drop at a time.

Once you've released a drop, let it dissipate for a moment to see what it does.

You can continue to add color until you achieve the tone you want, mixing in different colors as needed. It's important to remember that you can't remove color once you've added too much, but you can always add more if you don't have enough. Using too much color not only ruins the soap aesthetically, but may cause stains on washcloths and basins.

Step 5: Pour the Melted Base into the Mold

Different soapcrafters have different opinions about whether or not a mold should be sprayed with oil before it's used. If your mold is flexible enough, you probably won't need additional lubricant to remove the soap. If in doubt, experiment with using a very light spray of vegetable oil spray from a can or oil sprayer. You may even want to pat the inside of the mold with a paper towel after spraying it to remove any excess oil that

may pool on the mold. If you leave too much oil on the mold, your soap will feel greasy.

Once you've poured the soap into the mold, spray the surface very lightly with rubbing alcohol to remove any bubbles that may result from pouring.

If the soap starts to solidify before you have poured it, reheat it. Remelting doesn't hurt soap.

Opinions vary when it comes to deciding whether or not soap should be placed in a freezer or refrigerator to set. Some say it's perfectly fine to put the soap in the fridge, but not the freezer. Others say it's fine to use the freezer to speed the setting time, as long as you don't leave your soap in there for hours. Still others say soap should never go in the freezer because it may freeze entirely, causing it to crack and break into pieces when you try to cut it. Once again, experiment to find out what works for you.

Step 6: Unmold the Soap

Once your soap has thoroughly cooled and hardened, unmold it. It's ready to use right away.

If you have trouble releasing the soap from the mold, you can try several things. Run the mold under hot water to help the soap separate from the sides of the mold. Place it in the freezer for a short time, then remove it. As it warms, the temperature contrast helps the soap pop out.

CREATIVE SOAP COLORING

A handmade soap should appeal to all the senses. Sight, smell, and touch are all engaged, and some soaps even look good enough to eat! The color, scent, and texture work together to set a tone, so you'll want all these elements to be coordinated. Consider the emotional effect of the colors you choose. A soap featuring hot colors and a strong fragrance has an energizing effect, while a soap with cool colors and a refreshing scent is soothing. The following list provides some guidelines on colors and the moods they convey.

Cold Colors
Clean, refreshing

Blue
Blue-green
White

Cool Colors
Peaceful, calm, meditative

Violet
Pale blue
Pale green

Warm Colors
Comforting

Yellow
Yellow-orange
Light green

Hot Colors
Stimulating

Red
Red-orange
Hot pink

Earthy Colors
Grounding, homey

Brown
Dark green
Off-white

Romantic Colors
Peaceful, soothing

Pink
Peach
Lavender
Sky blue

A FRAGRANCE PRIMER

Smell is the most powerful of the five senses. The aroma of a batch of fresh-baked cookies can unconsciously bring back a wonderful childhood memory as clearly as if it had happened yesterday. A soap's fragrance (if it has one) should be evocative, too, and should work well in conjunction with its other elements: shape, color, and texture.

Creating fragrance has been compared to developing fine wine. Vintners choose different varieties of grapes to create the complicated, textured flavor that distinguishes one wine from another. Perfumers (and soapcrafters) use a similar process to blend different scents and create a memorable fragrance. Each fragrance has different characteristics and behaves differently when mixed with others. To identify different scents within a mix, perfumers refer to fragrances as "notes." In a fragrance recipe, the "high note" scent is the one that makes the first impression, while one with a more sustained effect is called a "middle note." A scent added for contrast is known as a "low note." In a typical fragrance blend, a citrusy scent (orange, lime, or lemon) would be the high note, something sweet such as vanilla, would constitute a middle note. A low note would be an earthy, contrasting scent, such as sandalwood or patchouli.

Check out the following list of fragrances and their characteristics. Although it's difficult to describe a scent, this guide will give you a starting point for thinking about fragrance mixing. While you won't be able to immediately sample an oil from an on-line supplier, natural food stores often have tester vials available. While playing around with fragrances, test your recipe on a paper towel rather than your skin. You'll get a truer sense of the smell, and it will be easier to distinguish between different fragrances. If you mix scents for hours on end, give your nose a break. Your ability to accurately identify fragrances diminishes over time and everything starts to smell the same.

Bergamot
Scent: sweet, citrusy, with a hint of floral
Effect: relaxing, refreshing
Complementary fragrances: rose, gardenia

Calendula Flower
Scent: light, herbal
Effect: cooling, soothing
Complementary fragrances: chamomile, lemongrass, ginger

Chamomile
Scent: fruity, herbal, nutty
Effect: relaxing, calming
Complementary fragrances: bergamot, lavender

Freesia
Scent: fresh, crisp, floral
Effect: stimulating
Complementary fragrances: lily of the valley, violet, rose, orange

Ginger
Scent: tart, citrusy
Effect: invigorating
Complementary fragrances: orange, lemon, lime, basil

Jasmine
Scent: sweet, delicate, floral
Effect: romantic, stimulating
Complementary fragrances: orange, apple, peach, vanilla

Lavender
Scent: floral, woody
Effect: relaxing (headache relieving)
Complementary fragrances: thyme, rosemary, lemongrass,

Lily of the Valley
Scent: strong, sweet floral
Effect: relaxing
Complementary fragrances: violet, lilac, gardenia

Patchouli
Scent: woody, spicy, sweet, musky
Effect: soothing, relaxing
Complementary fragrances: vanilla, jasmine, orange, sandalwood

Peppermint
Scent: crisp, clean
Effect: stimulating
Complementary fragrances: spearmint, lavender, chocolate

Pine
Scent: fresh, woody
Effect: uplifting
Complementary fragrances: frankincense, orange, lavender, myrrh

Rose
Scent: soft, rich floral
Effect: relaxing
Complementary fragrances: lilac, lavender

Rosemary
Scent: woody, crisp
Effect: stimulating
Complementary fragrances: lavender, lemon

Vanilla
Scent: sweet
Effect: uplifting
Complementary fragrances: almond, cinnamon, jasmine

Ylang-ylang
Scent: floral, sweet
Effect: stimulating
Complementary fragrances: lily, jasmine

YOUR FINISHED SOAP: PACKAGING

You may have noticed that a lot of homemade melt and pour soaps are wrapped in see-through cellophane bags or plastic wrap. Wrapping your final product serves two purposes—one functional, the other decorative, both important.

First, the functional. Glycerin naturally attracts moisture from the air, so if a glycerin-based soap is left out (especially in areas where there's a lot of humidity in the air), beads of moisture will form on the bar, a condition called "sweating." The sweat makes the soap slimy and unattractive, and causes it to deteriorate more quickly. To avoid this problem, wrap your soap in airtight plastic wrap, shrink wrap, or a cellophane bag. Wrapping your soap also preserves the strength of the fragrance, preventing it from dissipating too soon.

Wrapping your soap also gives it an extra element of interest, making it appeal to the eyes as well as the nose and skin. Use interesting papers, ribbons, and raffia. Attach something to the packaging to echo the theme of the soap. For example, if your soap features rose petals, hot glue a rose hip to the wrapping. If you've created an Asian-inspired bar, wrap it in inexpensive joss paper, or thread a Chinese coin through a strand of cord and wrap it around the package.

If you'll be giving the soap as a gift or selling it, be sure to create a label and list its ingredients so that the recipient will be aware of any potential allergens or irritants. The label is part of the appeal of the packaging, so spend some time creating a label that complements the soap and the rest of the packaging.

CLEANUP

For the same reason that you wrap your soap bars, you'll need to wrap any unused base in plastic wrap. If you don't, the base may start to sweat and deteriorate.

Since you're working with soap, cleanup should be easy! You may want to let your molds soak in water for a while to loosen any residue or dried soap, but you can put your containers and measuring cups in the dishwasher. Your molds can go in the dishwasher, too, if they are heat resistant.

ADDITIONAL TECHNIQUES

Once you've mastered the basic process, you can branch out to create soaps with more flair. The additional steps you'll take to create these soaps aren't necessarily more complicated, they're just a little extra work. As with simpler soaps, you'll learn through experience as you become familiar with these additional materials and methods.

Loaf Soaps

Loaf soaps are made in purchased or homemade loaf or tube molds. When cooled, a loaf soap is cut into separate slices. Loaf soaps give you more soap for the same amount of effort expended. There's really no special trick to making a loaf soap unless you want to layer it or embed items in it (keep reading!).

Double or Multicolored Soaps

This technique is easy to do with novelty molds, or even plain rectangles or circles. If you have a novelty mold that has a raised section, you can fill the raised area with a melted opaque base, then stop, let it cool, and fill the rest of the mold with clear base or any base with added color. To do this with a mold that doesn't have defined areas, pour a thin layer of base in a single color, let it cool, then pour base in a different color on top of it.

Suspending Items in Soap

If you want an additive to show up throughout your soap rather than restricting it to a certain area of the soap, you can suspend it in the mixture. After you've melted your base and added color and fragrance as desired, let it cool and thicken slightly, but not to the point that a film forms on top. Stir in your additive very slowly to avoid creating bubbles. If you do create bubbles, spray them away with a little alcohol. Pour your mixture slowly into the mold.

Embedding Items in Soap

To embed an item (such as a toy or another soap) inside a soap, pour a thin layer (about 1/4 inch [6 mm]) of soap on the bottom of your mold and let it cool. Spray the item to be embedded with alcohol. Place it on top of the soap layer you've already poured, then pour the rest of your base soap over it.

If you're going to place a soap inside another soap, follow these instructions (this is also called a "double mold" soap). Create a soap with a simple shape (square or rectangular) in one mold, and when it's ready, chop it into cubes. Spray the cubes with alcohol, place them in another mold, then pour melted base on top of them. Using contrasting colors, or a white opaque-based soap inside a clear-based soap, creates a dramatic look. There are infinite variations on this technique. Instead of cubes, you can create canes, grated soap curls, or circles, or embed a novelty-shape soap, such as a heart, inside another soap. You can also add colored slices of soap in larger block of clear soap.

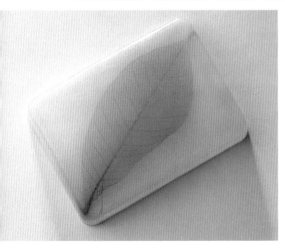

Layered Soaps

To layer a soap, pour a layer of melted base in one color or material (i.e. clear or opaque), then let it set (the first layer needs to be able to support the weight of the second). After the first layer has set, spray the top of the layer with a little alcohol, then add another layer in either a different base material or a different color of the same base material. You could even add a layer with an additive, like oatmeal. Don't forget the alcohol spray—if you do, the layers may not stick together and the soap may fall apart when you try to use it. Also, make sure the base you're pouring for the second layer has cooled a bit before you add it on. If it's too hot, it may break through the first layer. If your first layer hasn't cooled sufficiently before you add the second, color from the first layer may migrate into the second layer.

Rubber-stamped Soaps

You can use a rubber stamp to create an embossed look on your soap. Simply use a stamp that doesn't have a wooden back (available at craft stores), or carefully peel a stamp from its backing. Glue the stamp (face up) to the bottom of your mold with rubber cement. Pour your soap into the mold and let it set. When you remove the soap from the mold, use your fingernails or a pin to pry the stamp off the soap. If soap seeped around the edges of the stamp, leaving the impression messy, you can clean it up by scraping off the excess with your fingernail.

TROUBLESHOOTING

Making melt and pour soap seems easy, and *is* easy, but that doesn't mean it's a foolproof craft with guaranteed success the first time out. Until you get to know the materials well and have some experience under your belt, you may encounter some common challenges of the medium. The following is a list of situations you may encounter, and some possible explanations and solutions.

Common melt-and-pour soap problems, from left to right: soap that has not completely cooled and hardened, cloudy soap, bleeding colors, migrating color, sweating soap, cracked soap

Problem: Difficulty unmolding soap
Explanation and Solution
Your soap may not be cool and hard yet. Wait a few minutes longer. Try bending back the mold or sticking a knife around the edges to release it.

Before pouring your soap base, you may want to take the precaution of using a mold release, such as vegetable oil spray or petroleum jelly to ensure that your soap will unmold easily.

Problem: Bubbles in finished soap
Explanation and Solution
Stir your soap gently—vigorous stirring creates bubbles that are difficult to remove. Before your soap starts to cool, spray the surface of your soap with alcohol to remove bubbles that may have formed.

Problem: Cracking, breaking soap
Explanation and Solution
Cracks are caused by lack of moisture. Your soap could have lost moisture through overheating or by being placed in the freezer. You can remelt the soap, then add a little more soap base to regain some of the lost moisture.

Problem: Embedded soap is melting
Explanation and Solution
The soap that you poured over the embedded soap was too hot. Wait a few moments for the soap to cool slightly before adding melted base on top of soap embeds. Another problem might be that the embedded soap was sliced too thin. An embedded soap should be at least ⅛ inch (3mm) thick to protect it from melting.

Problem: Sweating soap
Explanation and Solution
Unwrapped soaps will often attract moisture, especially in areas where there's a lot of humidity in the air. Make sure to wrap your soap as soon as it has cooled and hardened. This problem may also occur when you use poor-quality soap base. If the problem continues after you've wrapped the soaps, try a different soap base.

Problem: Fragrance dissipates
Explanation and Solution
You may not be working with a cosmetic-grade fragrance. Your soap base could also be low quality, or you may have overheated the soap and caused the fragrance to burn off. Try using essential oils or fragrance oils.

Problem: Splits in layered soap
Explanation and Solution
Always spray the first layer with alcohol before pouring on a second layer—this encourages adhesion. Also, your first layer should still be slightly warm (but firm enough to support another layer) when the second is poured.

Problem: Bleeding colors
Explanation and Solution
This problem can happen when you use a poor-quality colorant (such as food coloring). Find out if your colorant is water-soluble. Water-soluble colorants are not effective in melt and pour soap.

Problem: Cloudy soap
Explanation and Solution
You probably overheated the soap, causing it to lose clarity. Always test your microwave temperatures before proceeding with a project to avoid overheating.

Celestial Soaps

Add a little sparkle to your bathroom with these gently twinkling celestial-shape soaps. Pearlescent powder is the trick to getting the stars and moon to shine. The molds are available through soapmaking suppliers or at craft stores.

Vegetable oil spray	Clear soap base
Moon and stars mold	White pearlescent powder
Sharp knife	Gold pearlescent powder
Cutting board	Spoon or stirring implement
Microwave-safe container	Moon and stars molds
Microwave oven	

1 Spray your mold with vegetable oil spray to make unmolding easier.

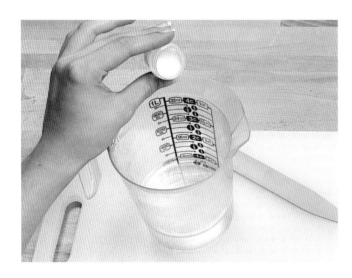

2 Cut and melt a small amount of clear soap base. Slowly stir in white pearlescent powder to suspend it throughout the mixture. Pour the mixture into the moon shape.

3 Cut and melt clear soap base. Stir in gold pearlescent powder and suspend it through the mixture.

4 Pour the clear mixture into the star shapes. Let cool and harden about 20 minutes (put the molds in the freezer to help them cool faster, if desired).

Spring Botanical Soap

A graceful skeletonized leaf lies deep inside this bar of soap, reminiscent of a fossil frozen beneath ice. Use clear and opaque soap bases and a mold with a rounded top and flat bottom to give this bar dimension and depth. Soft, subtle fragrances are suitable for this soap—try ylang-ylang, lily, or eucalyptus.

YOU WILL NEED

Clear soap base

Sharp knife

Cutting board

Microwave-safe container

Microwave oven

Skeletonized leaves for embedding*

Acrylic varnish (optional)

Rounded-top mold

Rubbing alcohol and sprayer

White opaque soap base

*If you use colored leaves, spray them with an acrylic varnish first so that the colors won't bleed into the soap.

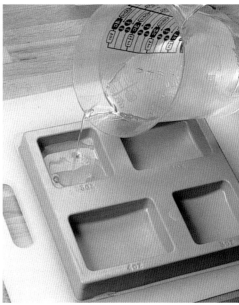

1 Cut and melt a small amount of clear base. Pour just enough to cover the bottom of the mold with a thin coat, about $\frac{1}{8}$ inch (3 mm) deep.

2 Spray the skeletonized leaves with a very thin coat of varnish if they have been treated with dyes.

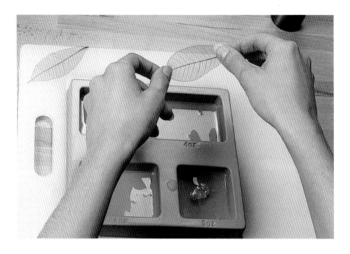

3 Wait until your first thin layer has cooled and set somewhat. Place a leaf into each mold.

4 Spray the top of the soap with alcohol.

5 Fill the rest of the mold with clear base, leaving about ⅛ inch (3 mm) of space at the top.

6 Cut and melt a small amount of opaque white base. Tint the soap base, if desired. Once the clear layer has cooled a bit, spray the soap with alcohol. Pour a very thin layer of opaque base on top of it. Let cool, harden, and unmold.

Gift from the Sea Soap

*This project gives you practice making three-dimensional soaps that
look great and feel great in the hand. This shell mold was made for
soapmaking, but you could also use molds for candle and candy-
making to achieve the same look. We created soaps from both
opaque and clear bases for contrast and added pearlescent powder
for extra shine.*

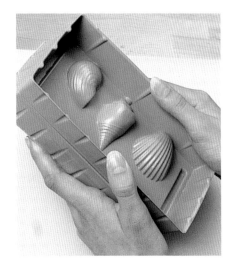

2 Coat both halves of your mold with vegetable oil spray. Click together the two parts of your three-dimensional mold.

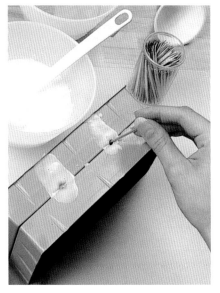

4 Insert a toothpick into the hole to clear any block and continue to fill the mold until it overflows slightly.

1 Separately cut and melt small amounts of both clear and white opaque soap bases. Slowly stir white powder into the white base and gold powder into the clear base to suspend it within the mixture.

3 Use your ladle and funnel to pour a single kind of soap base through the small opening in the top of the mold.

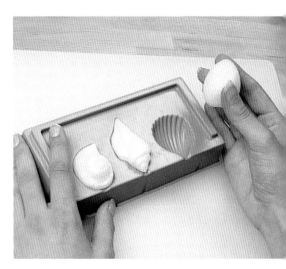

5 Wait at least 30 minutes for the soap to cool and harden, then pull apart the mold and remove the soaps.

Dragonfly Summer Soap

For this project, you'll practice making soaps with different defined color areas. You can achieve this look by pouring different color soap bases into the same mold—you just need to let the first color cool before adding the second one. The fresh colors used to make this soap are reminiscent of a summer day. If you add fragrance, use a fresh, summery scent.

White opaque soap base	Spoon
Clear soap base	Dragonfly mold
Sharp knife	Butter knife or other scraping implement
Cutting board	Stirring implement
Microwave-safe container	Blue soap colorant
Microwave oven	Rubbing alcohol and sprayer

Suggested fragrances: watermelon, cucumber, honeysuckle

1 Cut and melt a small amount of opaque soap base. Carefully spoon it into the dragonfly section of the mold.

3 Cut and melt enough clear soap base to fill the rectangular part of the mold. Add blue soap colorant and stir. Add fragrance if desired.

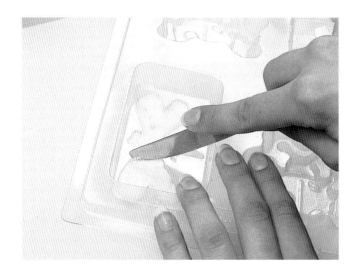

2 Once the soap has hardened, use a knife or other scraping implement to remove any that spilled outside the defined dragonfly area of the mold.

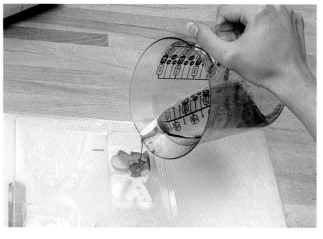

4 Spray the top of the dragonfly portion of the mold with alcohol. Once the clear blue mixture has cooled a little, pour it into the mold. Wait at least 30 minutes before unmolding.

Soap and Scrub

*Bath scrubbies make perfect embeds. You get the pleasure of using
the soap while enjoying the benefits of the scrubby inside it. After
your soap's gone, you've still got a great bath product to use for a
long time. If you choose to scent this soap, use an invigorating
scent or a soft, clean smell that complements the function
and color of the soap.*

Bath scrubby with handle	Cutting board
Deep-contoured clear mold	Microwave-safe container
Masking tape	Microwave oven
Clear soap base	Soap colorant in pastel colors
Sharp knife	Stirring implement or spoon

Suggested fragrances: baby powder, watermelon

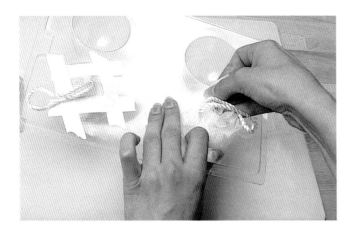

1 Place the scrubby in the mold. You'll need to push it down to fit. While holding it down, place strips of masking tape crisscrossed on top of the mold opening. You want the scrubby to be held down securely, but don't cover the whole opening with tape. You still need space to pour the soap base.

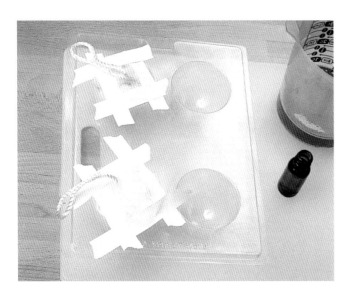

2 Cut and melt the soap base. Add colorant and fragrance if desired.

3 Pour the soap base slowly into the opening of the mold. Give it some time to seep down through the scrubby. Look through the bottom of the mold to make sure the soap is getting through and surrounding the scrubby (this is why it's important to use a see-through mold).

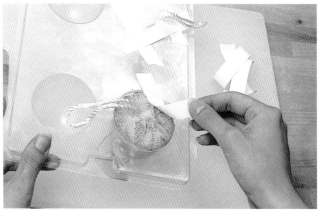

4 Let the soap cool and harden for at least 30 minutes (probably longer). Peel the tape off the top, and pull the soap out by the rope handle.

Shea Butter and Honey Loaf Soap

Shea butter is a rich moisturizing element that comes from the nut of the shea tree. Its creamy texture leaves the skin feeling soft and glowing. Combine shea butter and honey (another powerful moisturizer) and the result is a super moisture bar that pampers and heals dry skin. Make this soap in a simple loaf or emboss it with a rubber stamp, an easy trick that gives your soap a little more texture and appeal.

1 Cut and melt the clear soap base. Mix in about 2 tablespoons (29.5 ml) of honey and 2 tablespoons (29.5 ml) of shea butter.

2 Stir the mixture very gently and remove any clumps of either additive that may have formed.

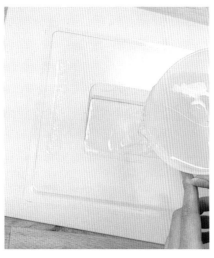

3 Place rags or dishtowels under the mold to stabilize it. Pour the mixture into the mold, stopping about ⅛ inch (3 mm) from the top. Let cool and harden, then spray with alcohol.

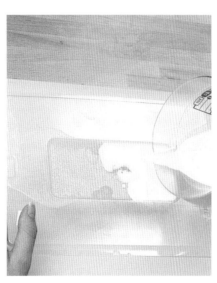

4 Cut and melt a small amount of white opaque base. Pour over the first layer. Let cool at least 30 minutes, then unmold. Cut into slices.

VARIATION

1 Place the bee rubber stamp face up in the center of the mold, then use rubber cement to secure it to the mold. Cut and melt white opaque base, then mix in the shea butter and honey. Pour a small amount of the mixture into the hexagonal mold to cover the stamp. Let it harden. Spray the thin layer with alcohol and then fill the mold to the top.

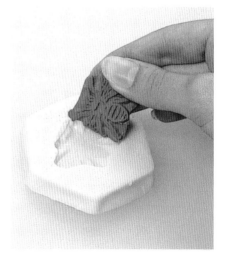

2 When the soap has cooled and hardened, unmold it. Peel the rubber stamp out of the soap with your fingernails. Scrape off any excess soap that covers the bee impression.

Cameo Soap

A cameo soap creates a wonderful touch of nostalgia—a perfect guest soap for those who appreciate the romance of the Victorian era. This look is very easy to achieve with a cameo mold, available from soapmaking suppliers and craft stores. The delicate look of this soap suggests a feminine fragrance like rose or gardenia.

YOU WILL NEED

White opaque soap base

Sharp knife

Cutting board

Microwave-safe container

Microwave oven

Spoon

Cameo mold

Dishtowels or rags

Butter knife or other scraping implement

Rubbing alcohol and sprayer

Mixing bowl

Stirring implement

Blue, red, and green soap colorant

Clear soap base (optional)

Suggested fragrances: rose, gardenia, lily of the valley

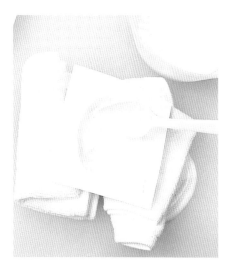

2 Set your mold on top of dishtowels or rags to stabilize it. Use a spoon to carefully pour the melted base into the raised cameo section of the mold, stopping when you get to the decorative portion. Let cool and harden for about 20 minutes (use the freezer to cool if desired). Scrape off any excess white soap that may have dripped outside of the raised section of the mold. Spray with alcohol.

3 Cut and melt more opaque base. In a separate container, mix blue soap colorant with just a drop of green and red to achieve a deep cornflower blue. Add fragrance if desired.

4 Make sure your white layer has cooled sufficiently before pouring the blue mixture, otherwise the color migrate; that is, the white could seep into the blue layer. Pour your blue mixture and let cool and harden for about 30 minutes.

VARIATION

For a nice contrast, try creating this soap with white opaque soap base in the raised section and a clear soap base in the decorative section.

1 Cut and melt the opaque base. This type of base comes in prescored blocks, making it easier to cut.

Pink Petals

*This beautiful, delicate soap couldn't be more feminine or romantic.
Pink pearlescent powder is suspended throughout the mix, and
crushed pink rose petals accent the bottom. A round or oval mold
complements this recipe—no hard edges. If you choose to add
fragrance, rose is your obvious choice.*

*Available at natural food stores

Suggested fragrance: rose, of course!

2 Steady your mold on top of rolled up towels or dishrags. Pour the mixture into the molds, leaving about ⅛ inch (3 mm) empty on the top. Let this layer cool and harden for at least 30 minutes.

4 Spray the top of the first layer with alcohol, then pour the opaque layer on top of it.

1 Cut and melt the clear soap base. Add pink soap colorant. Measure a small amount of pink pearlescent powder (about ½ teaspoon [2.4 ml]) and slowly stir it into the soap base to suspend it throughout the mixture.

3 Cut and melt a small amount of opaque base. Add a small amount of pink soap color and stir gently. Add rose fragrance if desired, then add crushed rose petals and mix.

5 Let the soap cool and harden for at least 30 minutes, then unmold.

Icy Clean Soap

*This soap combines a snowflake mold and icy blue colorant to create
a crisp, clean feeling. Sparkling glitter and pearlescent powder
suspended in the soap adds to the appeal. Add a fresh fragrance like
peppermint or wintergreen to give it extra kick.*

Clear soap base	Pearlescent powder or glitter
Sharp knife	Snowflake mold
Cutting board	Scraping implement
Spoon	Rubbing alcohol and sprayer
Microwave-safe container	Blue cosmetic grade glitter
Microwave oven	**Suggested fragrances: wintergreen, peppermint, pine**

1 Cut and melt the clear soap base. Mix in the pearlescent powder or glitter.

3 Melt more clear base and add in fragrance and blue colorant. When the soap has cooled slightly, slowly mix in blue glitter, being careful not to create bubbles as you stir.

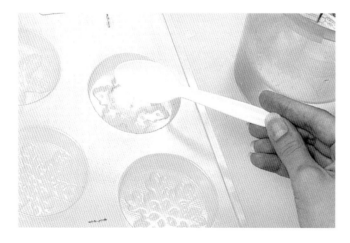

2 Spoon the soap mixture into the snowflake portion of the mold, stopping at the top where the mold levels out into an circle. Let cool and harden, about 15 minutes. Scrape out any excess soap that may have spilled into the level portion of the mold. Spray the top with rubbing alcohol.

4 Pour blue mixture into mold and let cool. Once hardened, unmold it.

Heart-Shape Soap Box and Jewels

A present within a present, this heart-shape box is made of soap, and contains a stash of hidden soap jewels. Making a soap box is no more complicated than making any other soap—you just need to be extra careful when unmolding. Suspend glitter in your soap jewels for added sparkle.

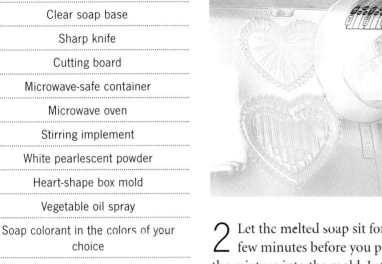

2 Let the melted soap sit for a few minutes before you pour the mixture into the mold. Let cool and harden for about 30 minutes. Unmold the box by pressing gently first around the sides, then on the bottom.

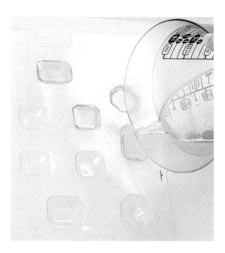

4 Pour the colored mixture into the jewel-shape molds.

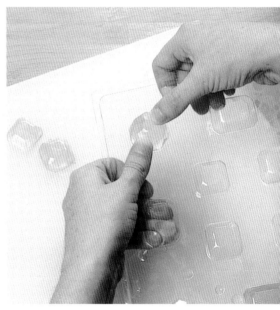

5 Let cool and harden about 20 minutes, then unmold.

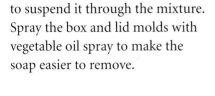

1 Cut and melt the clear soap base. Slowly stir in a few dashes of white pearlescent powder to suspend it through the mixture. Spray the box and lid molds with vegetable oil spray to make the soap easier to remove.

3 Cut and melt more clear base. Add a few drops of colorant and stir gently. Add a few dashes of glitter to the mixture and stir very slowly to suspend it.

Fleur-de-Lis Luxe Soap

This highly decorative soap sparkles on the inside and outside. Clear base is mixed with suspended pearlescent powder to create a subtle glow. On the outside, a layer of shiny gold or copper leaf is applied to give the soap a rich, luxurious look. The classic fleur-de-lis shape is a great mold for this sophisticated soap.

Sharp knife	Gold pearlescent powder
Cutting board	Fleur-de-lis mold
Microwave-safe container	Composition gold or copper leaf
Microwave oven	Craft knife
Spoon or stirring implement	Cotton ball or smooth cloth

1 Cut and melt the clear soap base. When it has cooled slightly, mix in the gold pearlescent powder, stirring very slowly to make sure the powder suspends throughout the mixture. Pour the mixture into the mold. Let it cool and harden for about 20 minutes, then unmold.

3 Use a craft knife to trim around the soap shape.

2 Cut a piece of leaf approximately the same size as your soap. Lay the leaf on the flat side of the soap.

4 Remove the loose leaf with a cotton ball or clean cloth.

Jeweled Raindrops

A playful paisley-shape mold is a great beginning for a colorful soap. The shape is reminiscent of refreshing raindrops. The embedded surprise is a sparkling sequin. Jewel-tone colors, such as pink and orange, and strong, stimulating fragrances combine to make this a fun gift or guest soap.

Clear soap base	Paisley mold
Sharp knife	Spoon or stirring implement
Cutting board	Sequins
Microwave-safe container	Rubbing alcohol and sprayer
Microwave oven	
Pink, yellow, and orange soap colorant	**Suggested fragrances: grapefruit, sandalwood, patchouli, clove**

1 Cut and melt your clear soap base.

3 Spray a sequin with alcohol. Place the sequin on top of the thin layer of soap.

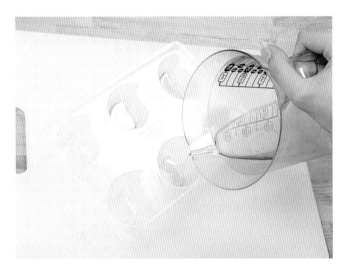

2 Add color and fragrance. Pour a thin layer of melted soap base into your mold—about ⅛ inch (3 mm) deep.

4 Fill the rest of the mold with melted base. You may need to remelt it if a film has started to form on the top. Let it cool and harden, then unmold.

Rose Soap Bouquet

This whimsical soap makes a lovely gift. A candy mold provides the shape and lollipop sticks serve as stems. Wrap the soap flowers in floral tape and add silk leaves for a charming presentation. This soap looks best, of course, when it's made by the dozen.

Clear soap base	Rose fragrance
Sharp knife	Rose candy mold
Cutting board	Lollipop sticks
Microwave-safe container	Butter knife
Microwave oven	Floral tape
Spoon or stirring implement	Scissors
Red soap colorant	Silk leaves

1 Cut and melt your soap base. Add red colorant and rose fragrance.

2 Place a lollipop stick at the end of each rosebud mold. The end of the stick should extend about $\frac{1}{8}$ inch (3 mm) inside the mold, with the rest hanging outside of it. Pour the soap into the mold and let it cool and harden.

3 When the soap is completely hard, unmold it. Use a butter knife to trim and cut off the leaves, leaving only the bud. If you spilled some soap on the "stems," don't worry about it. You'll be covering them up with floral tape.

4 Wrap floral tape around the stem. Add a small silk leaf, then continue to wrap around the rest of the stem.

Playful Bath Chain

This bath chain makes a great kid's soap. The bright colors and simple round shapes are appealing, and the cord is a fun way to tie them together. Use rainbow colors and fruity scents. To create the hole in the middle of each soap, use a hand drill or other sharp implement.

YOU WILL NEED

Clear soap base

Sharp knife

Cutting board

Microwave-safe container

Microwave oven

Soap colorant in jewel-tone colors

Stirring implement or spoon

Round mold*

Hand drill or other poking implement

Colorful cord

Tube mold (optional)

Aluminum foil (optional)

Rubber bands (optional)

*The designer used a throwaway plastic container from a sweet roll package. You can use whatever you have around the kitchen.

Suggested fragrances: apple, cantaloupe, watermelon, strawberry

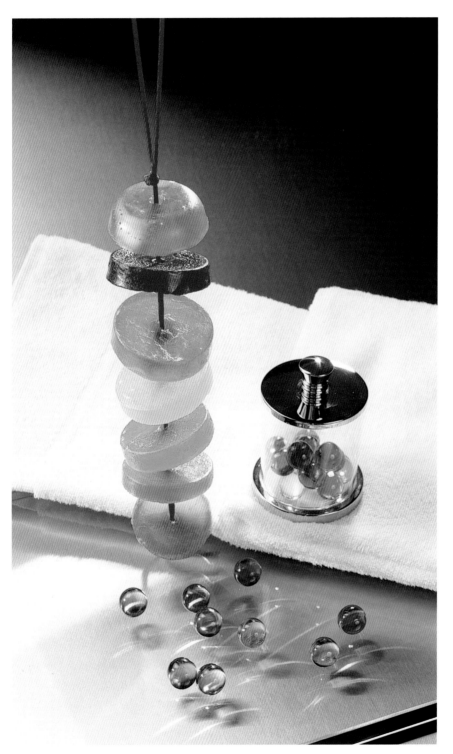

1 Cut and melt the clear soap base. Add color and scent.

2 Pour the mixture into the small round mold. Let cool and harden, then unmold. Make as many round soaps as you'd like for your chain.

3 Use a hand drill and bit or round implement with a pointed end to drill a hole in the center of each soap.

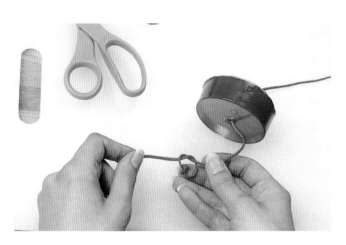

4 Pull the colorful cord through the center of the soap, then knot on both sides of the soap. Make another soap in a contrasting color using the same process and add it onto the cord. Continue adding soaps as desired.

VARIATION

You can also make a bath chain of soaps in the same color by using a tube mold.

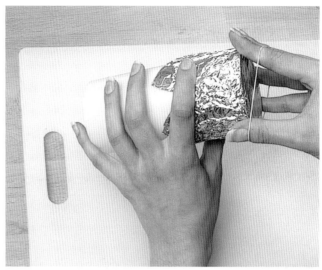

1 Cover one end of the tube with aluminum foil and secure the foil tightly with rubber bands. Melt, mix, and pour the soap into the tube mold and let it harden for 30 minutes or more (use the freezer to speed the process if desired).

2 Pull off the aluminum foil and push the soap out of the mold. Slice off the rough edges of the soap and cut the rest of the soap into slices, each about ½ inch (1.3 cm) thick.

Essential Elements Soap

Earth, air, fire, and water. Each of these soaps evokes the sense of one of the essential elements, and the Chinese character that represents the element is embedded inside. The characters are simply photocopied onto transparent acetate then layered in the soap. The colors and fragrance are up to you. We used red for fire, blue for water, green for earth, and clear for air.

Clip art images of Chinese characters	Microwave oven
Transparent acetate	Round or rectangular mold
Scissors	Rubbing alcohol and sprayer
Clear soap base	Spoon
Sharp knife	Blue, green, and red soap colors
Cutting board	Cosmetic grade glitter (optional)
Microwave-safe container	

Suggested fragrances: ylang-ylang, ginger, jasmine, orange, musk

1 Find images of Chinese characters for the essential elements. You can download the images from the Internet or use clip art. Photocopy the images onto transparent acetate and cut them out.

3 Once you have a thin, solid layer, lay the Chinese character in the mold, and spray with alcohol.

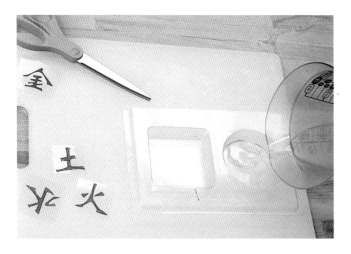

2 Cut and melt the clear soap base, and pour a thin layer of melted base into your molds. Let cool and harden somewhat.

4 Melt another batch of clear soap, then add color and fragrance if desired. If you wish, suspend glitter through the mixture by slowly stirring it in as the mixture cools slightly. Pour the colored layer into the mold over the transparency character. Let harden and unmold.

Citrus Loofah

A loofah sponge is ideal for exfoliating. Scrubbing with one leaves the skin glowing and refreshed. Use a loofah as a soap mold, and you've got a great bath accessory once the soap is gone. Citrus colors and fragrances such as orange, lemon, or lime give this soap a fresh, inviting feeling.

Purchased loofah sponge	Clear soap base
Sharp knife	Microwave-safe container
Cutting board	Microwave oven
Plastic cling wrap	Spoon
Rubber bands	Yellow, orange, and green soap colorant

Suggested fragrances: orange, lemon, lime

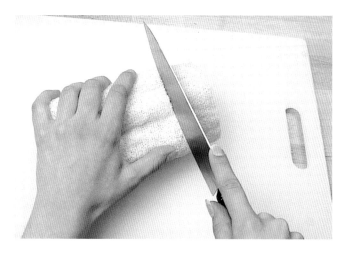

1 Using a sharp knife, cut your loofah sponge into pieces, each about 2 inches (5 cm) thick.

2 Wrap one end of each slice with plastic cling wrap and secure the plastic wrap in place with several rubber bands. You'll want the cling wrap to be very tightly attached to prevent the soap from leaking out the bottom.

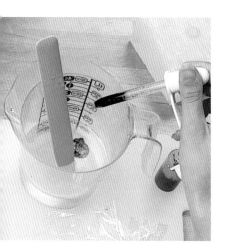

3 Cut and melt the clear soap base, then add fragrance and color.

4 Let the melted base cool slightly, then pour it into the holes in the loofah. Allow the soap to harden. Remove the wrap and trim the end with a butter knife if needed.

VARIATION

You can also make this soap with a small round loofah sponge (available in the cosmetics section of a drug store). Place the sponge in a circular mold, and then pour the remaining soap base over it. The result is a flat sponge coated in soap that's compact and great for travel.

Rainbow Cones

You can make a mold from just about any substance that's resistant to high temperatures. These cone-shape soaps were made from an acetate sheet mold that was taped together with masking tape. The shape was inspired by the paper cones that serve as drinking cups at water coolers (which can also be used as molds). These soaps fit nicely in the hand and make a wonderful bathroom display. Use jewel-tone colors and crisp scents for maximum impact.

YOU WILL NEED

Acetate sheet

Paper cones (optional)

Scissors

Vegetable oil spray

Masking tape

Clear soap base

Sharp knife

Cutting board

Microwave-safe container

Microwave oven

Soap colorant in jewel-tone colors

Stirring implement or spoon

Ladle or funnel

Wide-mouth jar or drinking glass

Suggested fragrances: ginger, lime, grapefruit, cinnamon, tangerine, verbena, mango

2 Form a cone shape from the cut acetate and tape it securely together at the side. Remember, you're going to be pouring hot liquid into this cone, so you need to make sure there won't be any leaks. Spray the inside of the cone with vegetable oil spray.

4 Allow the melted soap to cool slightly. Use a ladle or funnel to pour the melted base into the cone. Leave the cone inside the jar to cool and harden.

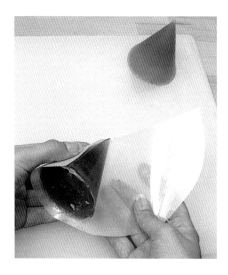

5 After about 20 minutes, peel off the masking tape to unmold.

1 If you can't find paper cones, create a cone shape from a sheet of acetate. Cut a circle from the sheet, then cut the circle down the center.

3 Cut and melt the clear soap base and add color and fragrance if desired. Place the cone upside down in a jar or drinking glass to stabilize it.

Arctic Dots

This soap evokes a cool, crisp feeling that comes from the contrast in colors and the cool, minty fragrance. For this easy embedding project, you need some sort of small round cutting tool. We used a cutter designed for polymer clay, but you could also try cake, pastry, or candy tools. It's fun to make this soap in pairs so nothing is wasted—one with blue embeds in clear and one with clear embeds in blue.

YOU WILL NEED

Clear soap base

Cutting board

Sharp knife

Small round clay or dough cutter*

Aluminum foil

Rubber bands

Stirring implement

Small funnel

Blue soap colorant

Microwave-safe container

Microwave oven

Rubbing alcohol and sprayer

Round mold

Vegetable oil spray

*Available at craft stores

Suggested fragrances: mint, wintergreen, peppermint, spearmint

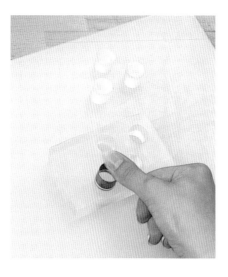

2 Press the clay cutter into a slice of soap base, extracting a round plug of soap. Continue removing plugs in a pattern of your choice.

3 Wrap aluminum foil around the bottom of the slice, securing it in place with a rubber band. Make sure the foil is tightly secured so the soap mixture doesn't run out the sides. Spray with alcohol.

4 Melt a small amount of clear base and add color and fragrance. Let it cool slightly. Use a funnel to pour the soap mixture into the holes created when you extracted the plugs in step 2. Let cool and harden, then unmold. If any of your colored mixture seeped, trim it off with a sharp knife.

5 Spray the circular mold with vegetable oil spray. Arrange the round soap plugs in the bottom. Spray the plugs with alcohol. Pour the remaining blue mixture (which should be slightly cooled, but still completely fluid) into the mold. Let cool and unmold.

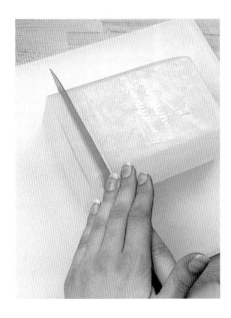

1 Slice the clear soap into as many ½-inch (1.3 cm) slices as you want.

Checkerboard Loaf

Once you're comfortable creating individual or layered soaps, try creating a loaf soap. You can slice it into separate bars, giving you much more soap for about the same amount of effort. We used two different kinds of soap base—clear and opaque white—to show how the same color looks when added to each base type. If you don't have a loaf mold or tin, you can create one with aluminum foil.

Clear soap base	Stirring implement or spoon
Sharp knife	Aluminum foil (optional)
Cutting board	Ladle
Microwave-safe container	Rubbing alcohol and sprayer
Mircowave oven	White opaque soap base
Orange soap colorant	Loaf mold

Suggested fragrances: peach, orange blossom

1 Cut and melt the clear base. Add colorant to desired shade. Form a ½-inch (1.3 cm) thick shallow mold by folding aluminum foil into a rectangle, then building up the sides. Make sure your mold is sturdy enough to hold liquid.

2 Once the soap has cooled and hardened, peel off the aluminum foil and cut the soap into long strips.

3 Arrange the orange strips in the bottom of the mold, and spray with alcohol. Leave some empty space between strips.

4 Cut and melt the opaque base. Add color and fragrance. Let it cool slightly. Use a ladle to pour the base over the first layer of strips. The base will fill the empty spaces you left in between layers. Wait until the first layer has cooled, then lay a second layer of orange strips above the first, alternating the pattern (make sure these strips have been sprayed with alcohol). Again, repeat the process of pouring the opaque base over the strips. If the base starts to harden, simply remelt it. Repeat the process of creating layers until you've reached the top of the mold. When the loaf has hardened, release it from the mold and cut it into slices.

Lemongrass Soap

Lemongrass has a potent, but not overpowering, citrusy scent, making it the perfect herb for soapmaking. Known for its antiseptic and cooling properties, it's also said to be an insect repellent. Test this soap during the summer and see what you think!

Clear soap base	Stirring implement
Sharp knife	Dried lemongrass
Cutting board	Oval-shape mold
Microwave-safe container	Dishtowels or rags for propping mold
Microwave oven	Dried calendula flower (optional)
Yellow soap colorant	

1 Cut and melt the clear soap base. Add yellow colorant and stir very gently to distribute it throughout the mixture.

2 Add about 2 tablespoons (30 g) of lemongrass to the mix, depending on the size of your soap mold.

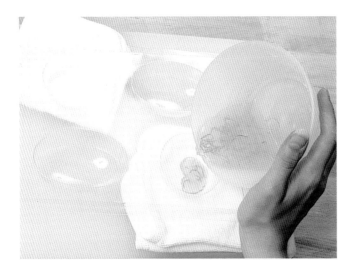

3 Prop your mold on dishtowels or rags to stabilize it. Pour the mixture slowly into the mold.

4 Let cool and harden for about 30 minutes, then unmold.

VARIATION

Use this same simple recipe, but add calendula flower instead of lemongrass to get a bit of green color and a sweet scent.

Honeybee Soap

A bee skep is an appealing shape for this charming soap, which is infused with the moisturizing power of honey. Sparkling highlights of gold pearlescent powder add a subtle glow. The honey provides a hint of fragrance, so there's no need for additional scent. Latex molds like the one used here are available through candlemaking suppliers and make unmolding a breeze.

1 Cut and melt the clear soap base. Add a few drops of honey—depending on the size of your mold, you probably won't need more than 1 teaspoon (5 ml) per soap.

2 Let the base cool slightly. Add a few dashes of pearlescent powder to the mix and stir very slowly to suspend the powder through the base.

3 Place your mold upside down in a wide-mouth jar to stabilize it.

4 Pour the melted base into the mold.

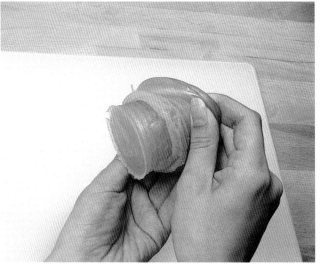

5 Allow the soap to cool. Peel back the mold to remove. Trim the excess dried soap from around the bottom of the soap.

Soothing Aloe and Nettle Soap

Aloe vera gel is known for its healing properties—it coats the skin and promotes rejuvenation, so it's great for cuts and burns. The nettle plant is known for its sting, but when its leaves are dried, they provide soap with a hint of green color and just the slightest leafy scent. This is an earthy, rejuvenating soap that's wonderful to use after a hard day's work in the garden.

YOU WILL NEED

Clear soap base	Aloe vera gel*
Sharp knife	Measuring spoons
Cutting board	Dried nettle leaves*
Microwave-safe container	Round-top mold
Microwave oven	*Available at natural food stores

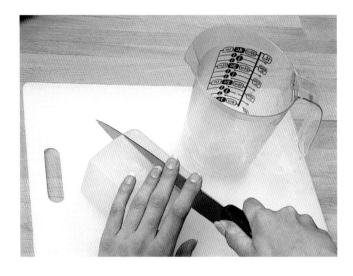

1 Cut and melt the clear base.

3 Dried nettles often come with stems that can be harsh and sharp. Remove the stems from the bag, and place a thin coat of nettle leaves on the bottom of the mold.

2 Measure around 4 tablespoons (60 g) of aloe vera gel (depending on the size of your mold) and spoon it into the melted base. Stir very slowly to dissolve the gel and make sure there are no clumps.

4 Pour the base into the mold over the nettle leaves. Don't worry if the leaves rise from the bottom and float throughout the soap—this makes for a more interesting look. Let cool and harden, then unmold.

Layered Herb Loaf

Lavender, rosemary, and calendula flowers are healing herbs which look great when embedded or suspended in a clear soap. The lavender provides a wonderful smell and a soft lilac color; rosemary is a pungent herb that gives soap a light green tint; and calendula flower smells sweet and has a warm yellow color. Combined in this loaf mold, they make a dramatic and naturally beautiful soap.

YOU WILL NEED

Clear soap base

Sharp knife

Cutting board

Microwave-safe container

Microwave oven

Stirring implement

Dried lavender*

Loaf mold

Rubbing alcohol and sprayer

Lavender fragrance or essential oil
(optional)

Dried rosemary*

Dried calendula flower*

Soap colorants (optional)

*Available at natural food stores

1 Cut and melt the clear base. Stir in a handful of dried lavender. If you want the lavender fragrance to be stronger, mix in a few drops of lavender fragrance or essential oil. Add colorant if desired.

2 Pour a thin layer of the mixture into the mold—about ¼ inch (6 mm) thick, depending on the size of your mold. Let cool and harden about 30 minutes (put in the freezer if necessary). Spray with a layer of alcohol.

5 Spray the layer with alcohol.

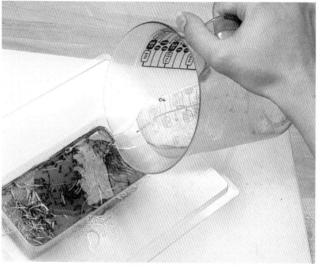

3 Cut and melt more clear soap base and add dried rosemary.

6 Cut and melt more clear base, then add dried calendula flower to the mix. Spray the layer with alcohol. Pour the mixture into the mold, stopping just short of the lip. Allow it to cool and harden, then unmold. Slice into bars, each about ½ inch (1.3 cm) thick.

4 Pour the rosemary layer, again about ¼ inch (6 mm) thick. Allow to cool and harden.

Gardener's Soap

After a day spent digging in the dirt, a gardener needs a good, strong soap to wash away the grit and grime. This hardworking soap features suspended oatmeal—great for exfoliating. It's made in a tube mold so you can loop a sturdy rope through the center and hang it over a garden faucet for convenience.

YOU WILL NEED

Ground oatmeal

Ground cornmeal

Food or coffee grinder (optional)

Ground coffee or red clay

Olive oil or vegetable oil spray

Aluminum foil

Rubber bands

Large tube mold

Skillet

Stove top

Olive oil soap base

Sharp knife

Cutting board

Microwave-safe container

Microwave oven

Small tube mold or PVC pipe

Putty or polymer clay

1 If your oatmeal, cornmeal, and coffee is not already ground, use a coffee or food grinder to prepare it. Toast the oatmeal in a skillet, using olive oil or vegetable oil spray as a lubricant.

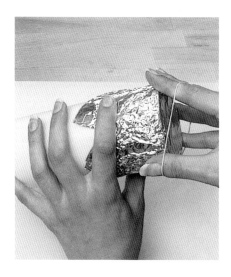

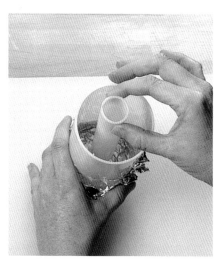

2 Wrap aluminum foil around the bottom of your large tube mold and secure it in place with rubber bands. Be sure to wrap it very tightly, or your mixture may seep out the bottom of the mold.

4 Create a plug of polymer clay or putty for the bottom of the small tube mold and insert it into the larger mold. Spray the interior of the mold with vegetable spray to make the soap removal easier. Pour the mixture into the large tube mold.

VARIATION

Use the same recipe to create massage bars (the soaps with raised bumps on the bottom), ovals, or squares. You can even use a bread mold (just be sure to spray it with vegetable oil first to ease removal later).

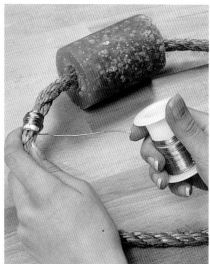

3 Cut and melt the olive oil base soap. Mix in your cornmeal, toasted oats, red clay or coffee, stirring very slowly to suspend the ingredients and avoid bubbles.

5 Once the soap has cooled for about an hour, remove the inner, then the outer, tube mold. Slice the soap into pieces if desired. Slide a sturdy rope through the center hole and secure it in place with wire (this prevents having to tie a big unwieldy knot in the rope).

Herbal Tea on Ice Soap

Herbal teas provide soap with not only color but light fragrance and the healing power of herbs. Infuse your soap with chamomile tea for a flowery scent and a light yellow color. Try raspberry for a touch of red and a tart fragrance. Lemon or mint teas are also great choices. Adding small clear glycerin embeds gives your soap a wonderful dimension and creates the illusion of ice cubes suspended in tea.

YOU WILL NEED

Clear soap base

Sharp knife

Cutting board

Tube mold

Aluminum foil

Rubber bands

Microwave-safe container

Microwave oven

Herbal tea bags

Spoon

Vegetable oil spray

Rubbing alcohol and sprayer

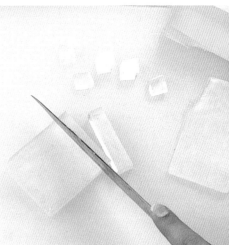

1 Melt the clear base. Let it cool and harden, then cut it into ¹/₂-inch (6 mm) chunks.

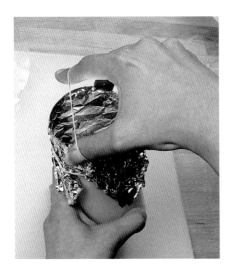

2 Cover the bottom of the tube mold with aluminum foil and secure it in place with rubber bands. Be sure to pull the rubber bands tightly so the melted base won't seep out of the bottom.

3 Cut more soap base and melt it in the microwave. Steep your tea bags in the melted base for a few minutes.

4 Press lightly on the tea bags to release the color. Reheat the mixture if necessary.

5 Spray your tube mold with vegetable oil spray to make it easier for the soap to release. Spray your clear chunks with alcohol and place some in the bottom of the mold. Pour some of the tea-infused melted soap on top of them. Repeat the process, adding more chunks, and pouring more base.

6 Let the mixture cool for 30 minutes or more. Remove the aluminum foil from the bottom of the mold.

7 Push the soap out from one end. If you have trouble releasing the soap, spray more vegetable oil around the opening.

8 Cut off the uneven ends of the soap, then cut the rest of the tube into slices, each about ½-inch (1.3 mm) thick.

Earth Clay Trio

Red, green, and bentonite clays are combined in this soap to give maximum absorption for oily skin. The clays cleanse and absorb toxins without drying, making this a great face soap. The deep contours of the mold allow for extra exfoliating power. As a variation, try creating a bar using a single type of clay, or cut chunks of soap in each clay type and embed them in an opaque base.

2 Once the soap has had time to cool, scrape off any mixture that hardened outside the contoured area. Spray the top with alcohol to prepare it for the next layer to be added.

4 Cut and melt another batch of soap base, then mix in bentonite clay to the same measurements you used with the other layers. Allow to cool at least 30 minutes, then unmold.

VARIATION

Try using a single color clay mixed with an opaque base in a very decorative mold.

1 Cut and melt your soap base. Mix in a few spoonfuls of powdered red clay—about 1 teaspoon (5 ml) per bar of soap. Place rolled towels or dishrags under the mold to balance it (this is necessary because of the contour of the mold). Carefully spoon the mixture into the deepest contours of the mold, stopping at the level area.

3 Cut and melt another batch of soap base. Mix in the green clay to the same measure you used for the red clay. Pour the clay mixture into the mold on top of the first layer. After this layer has cooled and hardened a bit, spray it with alcohol.

Green Tea Balls and Green Tea Infused Soap

Green tea is known for its healing and calming properties. Its rich green color and very delicate scent add a soothing element to soap. Because this soap has such a simple appearance, add creativity through your choice of molds. Use the same recipe in molds of different shapes and sizes and display them together, or wrap them in beautiful Asian paper and give them as a gift.

Clear soap base	Ladle
Sharp knife	Funnel
Cutting board	Green tea bags
Microwave-safe container	Three-dimensional ball mold
Microwave oven	Scraping
Stirring implement	Rectangular, square, and elliptical molds

1 Cut and melt your clear soap base. Open up a pouch of green tea and mix the contents in with the melted soap base, stirring slowly. Your mixture should turn dark green.

3 Cut and melt more clear base. This time, just insert the bag into the melted base and let steep. You will probably need to reheat and mix it slightly as it cools.

2 Snap the two parts of your three-dimensional ball mold together. Use a ladle and a funnel to pour the mixture into the mold, stopping when it starts to overflow. Scrape off any excess mixture that spills out. Let cool and harden.

4 Pour the mixture into square, rectangular or elliptical molds. Let cool and harden, then unmold.

Layered Sea Kelp Cake

Kelp is known for its deep cleaning and detoxifying properties—it naturally draws impurities from the skin. Combine it with powdered goat's milk, a moisturizing nutrient, and bentonite clay, a detoxifier, to create a cleansing soap that won't leave your skin dry. For this soap, the mold is simply a microwave-safe bowl—the same kind used for mixing and melting base. When the soap is hard and ready to use, cut it half, then divide into wedges for easy use.

1 Cut and melt the opaque soap base in a microwave container. Pour the melted base into another container and mix in about 2 tablespoons (30 g) of powdered kelp. Mix in a small amount of powdered goat's milk.

2 Pour a ½-inch (6 mm) layer of the mixture into the bottom of container mold. Let cool.

3 Cut and melt more soap base. Mix in a small amount of bentonite clay.

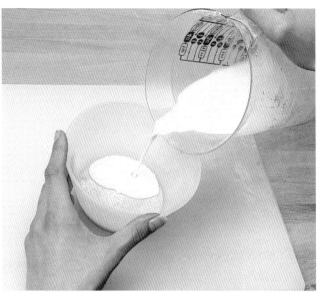

4 Spray the hardened layer with alcohol. Pour the mixture on top of the previous layer. Spray with alcohol and let cool. Continue alternating layers of white and green until you reach the top of the container.

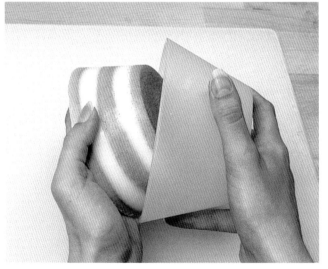

5 Let harden and cool for about an hour, and unmold.

Honey and Calendula Flower Soap

This soothing soap is full of rich ingredients that bathe the skin in moisture and leave a pleasant scent. Calendula flower is a healing herb with a sweet aroma and a warm yellow color. Honey is a natural moisturizer and cleanser. Because both additives infuse soap with color and fragrance, there's no need to add anything else.

Oval-shape mold	Microwave-safe container
Dishtowels or rags for propping mold	Microwave oven
White opaque soap base	Honey
Sharp knife	Ground (not powdered) calendula flower*
Cutting board	Stirring implement

*Available at natural food stores

1 Prop your mold with rags or dishtowels to hold it steady. Cut and melt the opaque soap base. Add honey to the melted mixture. You'll need just enough to thicken the mixture a bit and add color.

3 Pour the soap mixture into the molds on top of the calendula flower.

2 Place some calendula flower stems in the bottom of the mold—the amount you use is up to you, but you should at least try to cover the bottom of the mold.

4 Very gently and slowly mix the melted soap base and the calendula flower to suspend it throughout the soap. Let cool and harden, then unmold.

Clay Loaf

The deep cleansing power of three types of clay are combined in this appealing loaf soap. Red clay, white clay, and green clay gently exfoliate and draw toxins from the skin while leaving it silky smooth. This soap has an earthy, natural feel.

White opaque soap base	Spoon
Sharp knife	Aluminum foil
Cutting board	Butter knife or scraping implement
Microwave-safe container	Rubbing alcohol and sprayer
Microwave oven	Contoured mold
Powdered red clay, white, and green clays*	Dishtowels or rags for propping mold
Stirring implement	Loaf mold

*Available at natural food stores

1 Create a shallow rectangular mold by folding and shaping a piece of aluminum foil. Make sure your mold is sturdy enough to hold liquid (test it with water before using it). Cut and melt the opaque base, then mix it with a single type of clay and pour it into the foil mold. When it has cooled and hardened, peel off the foil. Repeat the process using a different type of clay.

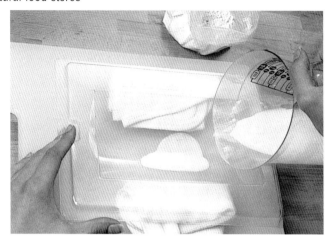

3 Cut and melt more opaque base, and mix in white clay. Pour a thin layer of this mixture into a loaf mold, using rolled up dishrags underneath to steady the mold.

2 When the soap has cooled and hardened, remove the foil. Cut each loaf soap into cubes.

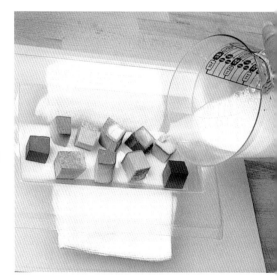

4 Once the thin bottom layer has cooled, spray your colored-clay soap chunks with alcohol and arrange them in the mold. Pour the remaining soap mixture on top of them (you may need to remelt if it has cooled too much). When your soap has cooled and hardened (a little over 30 minutes), unmold it, and cut it into slices, each about ¾-inch (1.9 cm) thick.

Acknowledgments

Designers Terry Taylor and Allison Smith created all the soaps in the book. Thanks, Terry and Allison, for your creativity, energy, enthusiasm, and style. As always, these two make a great team, and we appreciate their versatile talents. Thanks also to Terry for his expert advise on the Getting Started section.

Much praise to Megan Kirby, Chris Bryant, and Evan Bracken, who ran the photo shoot and dealt with the challenges and intricacies of photographing soap. What a tremendous job you did—the soaps look good enough to eat! Thanks also to Lorelei Buckley for her technical assistance on the photo shoot. Kathy Holmes, always the consummate professional, pulled the book together beautifully, and Barbara Zaretsky worked wonders with the cover. Thanks to Nicole Tuggle, our hand model, for her time and patience.

Most of all we'd like to thank Thomas Yaley, Jr., at *Yaley Enterprises,* and Carole Krinskey, at *Life of the Party,* for supplying the materials for all the soaps in this book. We loved working with all these wonderful products.

About the Designers

Allison Smith is a craft designer who lives in Asheville, North Carolina, with her husband and four wonderful children. She has been a contributing designer to over a dozen Lark Books, including *Garden Lighting for Outdoor Entertaining* (2002), *Girls' World: Making Cool Stuff for Your Friends, Your Room, and You* (2002), and *Gifts for Baby* (2003). When she's not creating, she enjoys reading, cooking, and traveling.

Terry Taylor is an artist, jewelry designer, and crafter who lives in Asheville, North Carolina. He is the author of *Weekend Crafter: Paper Crafts* (2002), and has contributed to dozens of Lark Books, including *The Book of Wizard Craft* (2000), *The Book of Wizard Parties* (2002), and *The Wizard's Book of Magic* (2003).

Index